AF445193

First Printing, 2023
Printed in the United States of America

ISBN 13: 979-8-9874213-0-7

Cohen, Marion Deutsche 1943 –

Published by agreement with Summerfield Publishing, d.b.a. New Plains Press,
Auburn, AL 36830, USA
newplainspress.com

Disturbing Shapes

Marion Deutsche Cohen

NewPlainsPress.com

Contents

Acknowledgements

"Worrying for Two" appeared in *Rat's Ass Review.*

"First Trump Nightmare" appeared in *Philadelphia Says "Not Our President"* (anthology)

"Bangles", "Great Fear of Death", and "Mousetraps "Circa 1940's" appeared in *Placeholder.*

"Trying to Explain Fear of Bugs" appeared in *The Wild Goose.*

"If You Like, Write about a Teacher..." and "Who Is Sylvia?" appeared in *Star 82.*

"Stuart Little" appeared in *The Broken Plate.*

"The Hole", "Fall Back", "If I Hadn't Skipped First Grade", and "Homeroom" appeared in *Hamline Lit.*

"End" appeared in *The American Mathematical Monthly.*

"Lives" will appear in *Evening Street Review.*

"Very Young" will appear in *Oyedrum.*

"The Colors of Everything" will appear in *Evening Street Review.*

Blurbs for Some of the Author's Recent Works

Praise for *The Project of Being Alive*:

"There is a great precision and correctness in Marion Cohen's work ... we live in a state of shared aloneness, and this is a book to keep at our bedside and, while reading by oneself not be alone at all." -- Mike Cohen, author of *Between the I's* and host of Poetry Aloud and Alive, at the Big Blue Marble Bookstore, Philadelphia, PA.

"This is an amazing collection in which dreams become part of the landscape ... Reality is always being tested ..." Hal Sirowitz (author of *Mother Said*, Crown)

"I savored her bounty of questions and absence of judgment–and her sense of astonishment." –Rachel Simon, author of *Riding the Bus with My Sister* and *Building A House with My Husband*

Praise for *Crossing the Equal Sign*:

"Marion is one of the few poets who can successfully explore the join between the literary and the mathematical sensibilities, and no one does it as well as she." –Jet Foncannon, Professor Emeritus of Mathematics, Drexel University

"highly original" –Anne Hudson, poetry editor of *Facets*

Praise for *The Fuss and the Fury*:

"This writer is a catalyst... she helps me give birth to a part of me that I realize needs to be birthed again." –Nancy Wainer, CPM (midwife, author, lecturer, educator), author of *Silent Knife: Cesarean Prevention and VBAC*

Praise for *Dirty Details: The Days and Nights of a Well Spouse*

"... a powerful meditation on the role of the well spouse in contemporary society ... I recommend it highly" –Christian Perring, Ph.D., in MentalHelp.net

Praise for *Chronic Progressive*:

"Each new publication of Marion Deutsche Cohen must be a cause for celebration!" –Lili Bita, author of *Sister of Darkness*

"Marion Cohen has never shied from honest talk ..." –Maggie Strong, author of *Mainstay: For the Well Spouse of the Chronically Ill* and founder of the Well Spouse Association

Praise for *The Discontinuity at the Waistline: My #MeToo Poems*:

"... Cohen's collection is powerful and empowering ..." –Beth O'Brien, *Mad Hatter Reviews*

PART I: Suspicious Proofs

Moon and Motion

We don't see the moon move.

All we see is, less than a minute ago it was behind the window frame.

What else moves in this way?

Not slow-motion movies, not turtles.

But the minute hand of a clock.

And growing, aging.

A baby's aging. We don't see babies age.

We know only that, at one day old, they look different from the
 previous day.

And Rachel Maddow looks younger in her clips of a year ago.

In early adolescence I had two theories of motion.

First: when an object moves it disappears from one place and appears
in another.

Second: There's no such things as fast and slow

fast just means the object moves more often.

Back to the moon:

It does kind of move some instances and not others.

And it does disappear from one place and appear in another.

E.g., We don't see it falling.

But it's no longer hovering above the church.

Instead it's dropped behind, lighting up the cloud above it.

And now that cloud has become darker.

The moon must be falling

further down.

Nature Might Not Know the Difference between Left and Right

But dreamers do.
Dreamers know which wall is leaning.
Dreamers know which door is pulling.
Dreamers know from which side
the shaded figure comes.
And babies do.
Babies know which arm is holding.
Babies know which hand is tickling.
Babies know which side
has the better milk.
And heel-diggers do.
Heel-diggers know which tooth must be poked.
Heel-diggers know which cheek must be puffed.
Heel-diggers know which heel
has to do the dig.
Things do not have to be symmetric.
In fact, things have got to be asymmetric.
Planes have to tilt.
Points have to twinkle.
That little knot
has got to squirm.

Middle-of-the-Night Lullaby

I must have been about eight when, sleeping over a friend's
house, I woke up in the middle of the night and didn't like
the "reflections" that the moon made so got up and started
struggling with the curtains, actually got up on the windowsill,
and her mother came in and asked what was wrong.

"What brings you here
"to the window, my child?
"Why at the window
"my pretty, my wild?"

"The curtain's a veil
"shielding something from me
"and the night is a face
"coming close to see."

"What is it here
"at the window, my child?
"Why at the window
"my pretty, my wild?"

"The stars up ahead
"are buzzing and crawling.
"The moon at the corner
"is blinking and calling."

"Oh, why on the sill
"are you standing, my child?
"Where are you climbing
"my pretty, my wild?"

"The curtains won't close
"and the shade won't stay.
"The night won't be black.
"It keeps being grey."

"Come, now, to bed.
"If you'll just close your eyes
"it won't trouble you
"what goes on in the skies."

"I tried that already
"and the night in my head
"that night won't be black.
"It keeps being red.

"O build me a room
"where the windows are naught.
"O build me a brain
"without any thought."

"Greeting Card Poem"

Whole afternoons in Woolworth, drugstores.
Queen of the Scene, Lord of the Board.
Such pretty pictures, such pretty words
such perfect rhythm, such perfect rhyme.
And then the cute-idea cards, cards like pamphlets.
"There are many kinds of mothers; some are fat and some are thin..."
and especially "Thank you once and thank you twice/ and thanks
again for being so nice."
Couldn't wait to flip from picture to words
and I'd get all-excited about it like thrift-shopping *now*.
When you bend over a piano you have to play.
When you bend over a notebook you have to write.
But when you bend over *these* slanted shelves
all you need do is bend further and further down.

Two is Worse than One

8

In the small room, on the floor towards the left, crawls a large roach. Then, in the sink, crawls another large roach.

That was a horror. Two is worse than one, more worse than you'd think, infinitely worse. In math it takes only two linearly independent vectors to generate, via linear combos, an infinity of them. So yeah, a whole plane of roaches. Whole floor, whole ceiling, or whole wall.

Three would be even worse.

How You Know the Writer's Block Is Over

What returns first is titles.
Sometimes more than one for the same poem.
Then last lines. And then fillers.
It's like learning to love again.
First you can love a flower
then an animal
finally someone in your own image.
And one morning you wake up remembering a dream.
The dream was intense
one of those stretching over the universe dreams.
The stretch was in a skew direction.
In fact, these days, many things are skew.
In the dream you arched like a rainbow
that had an end.

Dream Aged 14

Our mother keeps having more children.
Five, ten, twenty...
We never see her pregnant and we never see the babies.
There are no toys or photographs.
They grow up within the month and go seek their fortunes.
We go to the station and wave good-bye.
There are no suitcases or vacation visits.
We just drive down to the station.
Then we come back and she has another.
And she keeps having these children.
They pass through her body like little germs.
She hugs and cries by the railing.
Then she stares and nods down the tracks.
But we're her real children.
We stay on.

Worrying for Two

When we first fell in love he said, "*you* no longer have to worry
 about you. *I'll* worry about you."
So, he can take on my adult kids recovering from the long
 dying of their father. And I'll take on his adult kids recovering
from the long dying of his first marriage.
True, he can't grade my linear algebra papers.
And I can't translate all those pharmaceutical terms from Japanese
 to English.
But maybe he can dream my nightmares
give birth to dying babies
bring the wrong poems to a reading
lose purses again and again.
And maybe I can spin three times around in a strange train station
then walk in some arbitrary direction towards some arbitrary
 destination.
Yes, maybe I can be lost for him
and he can be lost for me.

Submitting '86

No
said yes.
Yes
said no.
Thirteen
took two.
Two didn't take thirteen.
Thirteen didn't say which two.

Still Life with Therapist

I am re-inhabiting each house
re-crossing each room
re-shuffling each foot.
I am re-being the four-year-old
on the floor with the crayons
that I kept snapping
and the scissors
that kept snapping me.
I am re-living that living room
and Kathy is with me.
Unheard, unseen, but oh, so felt.
Felt, say, on my right shoulder.
Such a Jiminy Cricket, such a tiny voice.
She is telling me, urging me.
About, say, my mother. "Don't let her say that.
"Don't let her say quite that."
And my father. I am re-being the thirteen-year-old
whom he did not pat on the back
nor send off to school dances with arms'-length adoration.
"Just leave him," says Kathy. "Leave him be. Leave him not be.
"Don't keep looking at him. Don't keep wondering about him.
"Don't keep trying, not even from time to time.
"Keep on being that brave little soldier.
"And know," she concludes, "know you're doing it. Know you're a
    soldier. Know you're brave."
She's my teacher, my grader.

My diary, my publisher.
She's all fourteen angels.
My theorem and my proof.
She's the little birdie that tells me.
The little birdie that asks me.
She lives and re-lives me and tells me to know.

End

They say we begin with answers and end with questions but
  mathematicians begin with questions and end with the same
  questions.
Are formulas coincidences?
Are proofs coincidences?
Especially when the proof is long. Long proofs are suspicious.
A proof should be one step. A thing happens for only one reason.
Are algebraic identities coincidences?
When something cancels out, is that a coincidence?
What exactly are the questions?
We begin with questions and end with nothing.
Just a bunch of theorems. Just a bunch of proofs.

Trying to Explain Fear of Bugs

Whenever a speck is bigger or darker than you remember, you panic,
  gather as many of your valuables as you can, leaving behind
  what you must.
On the skin of your back is a dark-brown furry benign growth an inch
  and a half in diameter.
You're afraid to look at it.
Once, on the black floor of the shower, you saw a raised spot
  that was even blacker and slowly moving.
You reached for one of your shoes.
Somebody said, "The thing is, they're not supposed to be indoors."
But if, while walking along early evening, you see something on
  the sidewalk scurry across...
well, they don't belong outdoors either. Or else *you* don't belong.

The Fury of First Sopranos

"This singing / is a kind of dying..."
Anne Sexton, "The Fury of Guitars and Sopranos"

This singing
is a kind of flirting
a gathering of hoops and parasols
a fluttering behind lace fans.
This trilling
is a kind of beckoning.
And this group-flirt is a shouting
a shouting from a safe place.
This room
is a kind of classroom
with a teacher
and rules
and plenty, plenty of mischief.
This giggling
is a kind of belonging
and this belonging
is something to need.
Yes, this singing
is a kind of living
a youthen-ing
a gardening
a ring of bright water.
Alto is too steady.

Alto is too shaped.
That warbling
is not a chirping.
Bass is like drums
not quite music at all.
Bass is like more of your own heartbeat
more of your own guts.
But first soprano is not like ultrasound
not like a hissing radiator
not like mice along the edges.
First soprano still has the tune.
First soprano still has the song.
First soprano is first.
First soprano is most.
Sop means top
the flight of the best birds.
And so here I stand
high and mighty
five foot nine
and high A-flat.
First soprano identified.
First soprano and proud.
"Glory to God [or to myself] in the highest."
This standing
is a kind of existing.
A real girl.
A real woman.
High A
and long E.
A real first soprano.
Female
and real.

Fear Itself

1. The dream seemed innocent enough. So why are you think-ing, "I need to cuddle but first I have to make sure he's not a monster"? Why am you checking his face, then through the blanket, making sure his feet aren't lower than they're sup-posed to be? And why, then, are you checking all around? Making sure the *objects* aren't monsters? That chair, various lamps, even your newly-acquired thrift-store black skirts and tops?
   Freud was righter than he wanted to be. Things aren't even close to what they seem. Abstract things, too, like your latest poem. They're all a single enemy, all your undoing. They have been getting ready, getting ready all along. *That's* what's been going on, all along.
2. This morning you wake up quickly and check the time. Is it four-thirty or twenty after six? Indeed, it's the latter, a good thing, almost seven hours' sleep, straight through the night. But the minute hand is longer than natural. It extends beyond the 4, beyond the field of the clock's inside, beyond the clock itself. It pierces through the glass, 'way out of its universe, as will we all, unwillingly, break out of ours.

The Five Stages

First came denial
nice and numb.
Then came bargaining.
That was dumb.
Then came anger.
Mostly you wept.
Then came depression.
Mostly you slept.
They come and they go.
They loaf and they strut.
And here comes acceptance.
Okay, NOW what?

Troubles after Sixty

1. The Trouble with Weekends:
   Sunday's not a weekend day
   because we have to get to sleep early to be up for Monday.
   And Saturday's not a weekend day
   because we know the next day's Sunday.
   Even Friday
   smacks of Saturday.
   Weekends are dead, or maybe only sick.
   They need rest, relaxation, and a very good doctor.
2. The Trouble with Vacations:
   We don't get weekends.
   In particular, we don't get Fridays.
   Today is the first day of the rest of the vacation
   until it becomes the last.
3. The Trouble with Retirement:
   We spent our childhoods convincing ourselves we still had enough childhood left. Then we spent our weekends convincing ourselves we still had enough weekend left. And we spent our vacations convincing ourselves we still had enough vacation left. Now we don't have childhoods, weekends, or vacations and we spend our lives convincing ourselves we still have enough life left. We know darn well we don't.

Dreams for Two

- For the first time in decades I have a flying dream.
  I never did tell him I could fly.
  "Look," I call out to him. "See? It's so easy."
  O'er trees, wires, hills, dales I show off my prowess.
  Then I wave down. But he's not there.
  He's up here with me. Yup, he can fly, too.
  Hey, we can both fly, what fun!
  But then, it's also a little scary.
  We'd better get back down.
- Me one morning: I just had yet another dream about going back
    to college.
  He: So did I. And it was finals week and I hadn't attended classes
    all term.
  Me: I can top that. At least you registered in the first place.
- After seven years we finally dream about each other.
  He, that he leaves objects around the house and I complain.
  I also inform him that I don't like his beard.
  And I... only that he's there, in whatever life I'm dreaming.
  Or not there, conspicuously absent leaving me unhappily alone
  with but some vague thought of him.
  How did you feel, I ask, when I didn't like your beard?
  "Disappointment," he answers.
  "Good," I say.
- I have an excuse to keep dreaming I go back to grad school.
  Real-life grad school didn't go quite right.
  But he has no such excuse.

So where does he get off going back?
There aren't enough back-to-grad-school dreams to go around.
And I need them more.
* This is my back-to-school dream.
But he's taking this course, too.
And it's probably a history course, or current events.
At any rate, he's way ahead of me.
For example, he arrived fifteen minutes ago
and he's been showing up all term.
Plus, he knows all the answers.
He seems to be teacher's pet.
During the break I shrug. "I don't get any o' this. I might as well
	go home."
And he doesn't stop me.
He's busy chatting with the teacher and a small group of other
	teacher's pets.
Yes, this is my dream.
But he's calling the shots.
* He dreams we go out to lunch together but then I say I don't like
the restaurant he picked so we decide to eat separately.
And I dream we're at one of his out-of-state conferences and it's
just after breakfast and
we forget to make plans where to meet for dinner.
But then we just happen to run into each other around lunchtime.
But then we forget to make plans again.
We run into each other two more times and keep forgetting to
make those plans.
* He dreams he never met me so he's never been loved.
But over the radio he hears a sweet sad song.
"I HAVE that song.
"Somewhere in my CD collection is that song."
So he hits his CD racks one after another in mad pursuit.

Instead of being loved
he'll settle for a song.
Whereas, when I dream I've never met him it's not a matter
  of songs.
It's a man I'm in mad pursuit of.
In those dreams the men have all broken up with me.
Sometimes there's a new possibility
but he's already growing cold
or he's so fat I can't fit my arms around him.
And I don't have a song. I don't even have a song.

About the Positive Integers

Most math-things number either infinity or one, non-unique usually means infinite. That's why polynomials are special, with their n roots. And the five platonic solids. And the only consecutive perfect powers are eight and nine. Also, there might be a first even number that's not the sum of two primes.

Yes, every number is interesting because the first *un*interesting number would have to be interesting in that way. But what about the *second* uninteresting number, or the third? The truly uninteresting numbers might be something *other* than interesting, something we might need. Yeah, we need at least some uninteresting numbers. Because maybe we're tired of interesting, maybe we want something more relaxing like just-plain beautiful, maybe just-plain loving. Maybe we want to be loved without having to be interesting. A friend once said, "Just bring wine to the party. You don't have to always be interesting."

And numbers don't have to be interesting. When Ramanujan said every integer was a personal friend of his in some way, he meant it, he meant even if he came across one that was uninteresting he would still consider it a friend. He never encountered any non-friend, he didn't leave anybody out.

Please

In "Incredible People" there was a baby
seemed normal
until the thirtieth day
then suddenly died.
They investigated.
It had no brain.
But it couldn't have smiled.
And it didn't flex.
And it didn't look up at its mother
with morning-glory eyes.
And it didn't breastfeed.
No, it couldn't have breastfed.
You can't pretend to flex.
You can't pretend to breastfeed.
There are some deeds
some words
oh please, there has to be something.

Schubert's Trout: The Song

I don't sing the third verse.
Never. Or never yet.
I refuse to admit it. Not out loud.
I don't know the words, don't know the melody.
I will not learn them.
I will not go gentle into that bad night.
I've sung many sad songs but not that third verse.
Only the first two. All around the town.
Only the first two. Sometimes again and again.

Three Theories of Everything

- The Same Things

  In each parallel universe only one person can be conscious. Dually, each person can be conscious in only one universe. However, in all the parallel universes the same things happen. So it's as though we're all together.

  Or maybe we're actually all together. Maybe that's what being together means. It means the same things happen according to us all.

- Recipe for Reality

  Take all the parallel universes in the previous parable and superimpose them. Since they're all the same except for the consciousnesses, all is well, nothing is unwell.

- Describing Reality

  It's like every function is some possibly-infinite linear combination of characteristic functions. It's like every vector is some linear combo of characteristic functions on singletons. Just take all the characteristic functions, some more than once, and pile them on top of one another. That reality is as good as any.

My Choice Today

There lies before me
math and poems.
I want the math more
but it's riskier.
If I take up the poems, guaranteed.
But math.
Sometimes the equation I begin with turns out to be the one I
    end with.
And sometimes that doesn't lead to ideas.
I look at the math.
I long for the math.
But, at least today
I am afraid.

The Music at the End of the Dream

It is not Beethoven.
It is only Mozart.
So why this racing, this escalating, why this flyaway panic?
Why these sharps and no flats, why these scales disguised as glissandos?
Why is the melody disappearing?
Why is this dream playing Mozart when it means Beethoven?
Why is it trying to make Beethoven be Mozart?
Why doesn't it just admit it's Beethoven?
Is Mozart pretending to be Beethoven
or the other way around?

Post-Partum Paradoxes

I am the only woman to have a baby.
And each of my sister women on the floor is the only woman to
    have a baby.
This is the best day of my life.
Now, how often have I said that?
I want this baby to be this baby.
But I also want this baby to be my previous baby.
I'm soooo happy.
But I look tired, messy, quiet, mostly tired.
I call him Beauty but that doesn't say it.
I need Binky, Dewdrop, Rosebud.
And I will soon have to get used to ordinary beauty.
I will have to get used to ordinary paradoxes.
Nazi women have had babies.
That might be the biggest paradox of all.

1985

Childhood

32

Yankees vs. Dodgers was like Democrats vs. Republicans.
They were things people kept talking about.
Parents, other kids, they all kept throwing around proper nouns.
Captain Video was another. I couldn't make myself want to watch
    Captain Video.
I didn't get Earth, how would I get outer space?
I wasn't all that popular so how would I know popular culture?
Parents at the supper table
neighborhood kids running around the battlefields of our back
    and front yards...
why was everybody speaking proper nouns?
Why couldn't everything just be lower-case?

Various Animals

conversation about the poem "Geese" by Agi Mishol, in my
course Mathematics in Literature

Some students like spiders. Some like whales. And Carly likes snakes and lizards. But even Carly doesn't like geese.

Some of us are okay with geese at a distance. But nobody likes geese up close. "Ew, yuk," we say, and Cory adds, "Their little teeth. And their slithery tongues." For every disturbing shape, meaning disturbing to somebody, there just might be an animal of that shape. Ew. yuk.

Schubert Songs I Won't Sing

34

Oh, I'll sing the beginnings.
But when they turn sad
too definitely sad...
I refuse. I deny.
Sometimes it's the last verse
sometimes it's the last line
and, for one song, it's only the last word.
And I won't say what that word is
or what the song is.
Not only won't I sing, I won't say.

Baby Steps

Today as he counts we sit with him.
We massage, sway, make eye contact.
We're his labor coach.
We count the contractions, or we count something.
Together and gently we take each separate
each as it comes
until he says he's had enough, it was just false labor.
Another time he'll have real labor.
We'll sit with him again, breathe and sway.
We'll count to the end, or far enough.
We'll be his doula, we'll help with the babies.
We'll be his blessingway, we'll pass them around
hold and admire each brand new one.
Then we'll hand them back
to him, the new mother.
Silent and respectful, we'll watch as he bonds
as he bonds with each
each unique and precious one
And each two, each three, each twelve, each fourteen
and whatever comes after twenty-nine.

1986

A Mathematical Theory of Literature

Any piece of fiction, no matter how long, is finite. The ending is the main theorem. And the author, via intuition or whim, has decided upon a set of axioms. Axioms don't need to be proven.

Kurt Goedel's math dissertation says, no matter how many axioms we add, not every true theorem can be proven, though adding axioms can help prove some particular theorem. Readers of a story would like to deduce, from the author's axioms, more details about the main theorem, would like to know more about the ending. They would like to know at least some of these undecidables. But that can't happen. Not without adding new axioms. And the author didn't.

Instead of Kerin

dream, 2020

Aged 77, I'm pregnant and this time the twist is, the doctors have somehow figured out how to make the pregnancy go the same way as the Kerin pregnancy, except at the very end they'd do a C-Section so the baby would live. What should I name the baby? Probably not Kerin but maybe something *like* Kerin, like a second Kerin, maybe KerEn with both e's like I wish I'd called the first Kerin, the one who died.

When I woke up I thought of a few names. Meta-Kerin, which is the title of one of my poems, and also "Instead of Kerin." Yeah, Instead of Kerin, but that's too long, maybe there's some other language where Instead of Kerin would be shorter.

So now instead of "Instead of Kerin" for a baby, I'm using "Instead of Kerin" for a poem. Yeah, that's a good name for a *poem*.

Foods to Fear

In kindergarten I was afraid of oatmeal
afraid they'd make me eat it.
It looked like throw-up.
I was also afraid of ice cream
afraid they'd make me eat it.
It turned liquid too quickly.
In fifth grade I wasn't afraid of Campbells' tomato soup and
macaroni with little cubes of Velveeta
until I threw it up.
It got all mixed together with my guts and the floor.
And I was afraid of squash because of its name
and canned peas, too slimy
and sour cream, and cottage cheese.
When I was a teenager, my mother started serving salad.
I was used to separately-cut-up celery and carrots.
I was afraid of salad, so I ate it without dressing.
Now I'm afraid only of squid (its texture too unexpected)
and soy milk (everything it's in tastes like it and only it)
and yogurt that isn't raita
and baked beans that aren't Heinz.
O yeah, and oatmeal (See above.
See directly above.)

First Trump Nightmare, November 2016

Somewhere, somehow, he and she are taking a walk.
He's confiding in her, telling her he killed a man, killed him
    because he didn't like him.
She loves being confided in but this time she's afraid.
She knows, in a matter of minutes, his voice will turn sadistic
as it says, "Now, how will I know you won't tell anyone?"
Yes indeed, how will he know? And in whom will he confide next?

The Birth of My Fourth Baby

We have photos.
I'm neither smiling nor straining because I'm sleeping.
My face is numb. I look dead.
It's sad that I'm giving birth and looking dead.
But it's happy that I'm giving birth to a baby who didn't die.
Sixteen months earlier I looked alive while giving birth to Kerin.
I'd rather look dead and give birth to life
than look alive and give birth to death.
Two and a half feet away was live Baby Bret.
And a couple hours later my face looked like it was supposed to.
We have photos of that, too.

Bangles

Ample, firm, pudgy, dramatic
and visible from any distance.
They're the only bracelets I wear.
Lately, though, there's been a problem:
they keep touching some part of my arm.
They make that part feel annoyed.
And if I raise my arm
keep it vertical
they touch that entire cross-section.
If I lower my arm (upside-down vertical)
they sit on my hand like water.
They won't leave my hand alone.
They make my arm tired.
They'll give it gangrene.
There's no good position for that arm.
But that's only lately.
Am I getting too old for bangles?
Do I have to start wearing those twiddly, weak, insipid,
    museum-type bracelets?
The kind you can barely see?
The kind you can barely touch?

Stamp Collecting

The other kids went for commemoratives, first-day covers,
    cancellation errors
and they divided their albums according to country and decades.
But my sister and I marked our sections birds, trees, dogs, trains.
My specialty was children, two pages of children.
The purple boy in a cloak surrounded, all eight sides, by perky
    little sparrows.
The red girl in kerchief and flowy dress talking to two
    perpendicular peacocks.
And the blue one, a circle of children, singing children, dancing
    children, under and around a wiry smiley sun.
The neighborhood came at us with page upon page of dark-green
    masculine heads
brown government buildings
offices
large tables
machines
shields.
We'd look away, would never trade
had no desire to own those dull little rectangles
newspapers scraps
encyclopedia illustrations
miniature, withered dollar bills.

Still

At 75 I'm, yes, still teaching
still publishing
still singing
still playing piano
and galavanting from thrift to thrift store.
And one other thing:
I'm still not believing I won't ever again be preg.
I wouldn't be surprised, just wouldn't
if I noticed my stomach increasingly protruding
and if that wasn't a dream.
Wouldn't be surprised and wouldn't be upset.
Nine pregnancies, five births, four upbringings have satisfied me.
I'm not craving pregnancy
don't feel I have to be preg.
But I'd be overjoyed
and I'd, yes, keep it
comb the thrifts for tiny stretchies
try for a VBAC
galavant with the baby carriage
again, and still.

Homeless Cat

It's being fed and petted by a homeless person.
It's lapping away at plenty of food.
"I've seen homeless dogs," someone says
"but this is the first homeless cat."
Cat, dog, makes no difference.
Homeless pets all get us in the same way.

Curlers: 1950s, 60s

I don't know why I thought I needed them, they didn't curl very much and only for half a day. I didn't really want curls, anyway, just wanted my hair to make up its mind, curly or straight, pageboy or flip, just wanted it all going the same way.

And they were uncomfortable to sleep in. I tried to arrange portions of the pillow in the spaces between them. Years later I discovered I could use just one big one, top of my head, I didn't sleep on the top of my head. And then I got the idea of using just my head itself, head as curler, I wound my hair either direction, held it in place with a towel.

And that eventually worked its way into none at all, only a hair-straightening treatment, by then I wanted it all straight. Fifty years later, if only I had more hair. But I won't use Rogaine, am happy enough with my hair, and more proud than thankful that it's mostly not grey except at certain choice angles. I also have a goodly supply of hats

from which my hair sort of sprinkles, like in the back pages of some fashion mags, little dots of skybluepink sunlight refractions, especially when it's arranged 'way in front, grazing each cheek, framing my face if not my head, and I need a hat to help this framing, to supplement my hair, which by the way is still partly curly and partly straight but now that's okay.

Great Fear of Death

We cannot believe our bodies won't mind being cremated, and
    then ashes, scattered or not.
We cannot believe our bodies won't feel it
will no longer have minds and consciousness.
On our deathbeds, will we think about that? We hope we won't.
We'll be, maybe, in a hospital, having what's known as a peaceful dying
everyone doing their best for our bodies – morphine, massaging
and loving, even if none of them are our loved or loving ones.
We hope we won't think for even a smidgeon
that all that very best for our bodies
will, once dying has become death, turn into the very worst.
We cannot believe the sheet won't suffocate
nor the wheeling out of the room frighten
nor the rest of it
the rest of it.
We hope, on our deathbeds, we forget all that.
We're not forgetting now but we hope we forget later
hope we forget lat*est*
our very latest of all.

Mousetraps Circa 1940s

Sometimes my parents heard mice scurrying about in the attic.
They set traps, the old-fashioned kind, the kind that snap on tails.
Whenever one of them worked my father would put the whole
    kit 'n' caboodle in a paper bag and head for the fields.
Once he took me with him. I watched him open the bag and
    then the trap.
The mouse scampered out among the wildflowers.
"'Bye, little mousie," my father crooned. "Bye bye, mousie."
The straight line segment that the mouse scampered along got
    longer and longer.
I guessed it knew where it was going.

About the New Typewriter, 1970s

"What does it do?" writer-friend Julie Blackwoman

It doesn't publish.
On the other hand, it doesn't reject.
It's not a workshop. It doesn't exclaim "O Wow."
On the other hand, it doesn't pout, "Well, I like the second
    word of the tenth line."
It's not an editor. It doesn't say, "We're going to have to DO
    something about this."
Nor, on the other hand, "Perhaps you should consider a wider
    range of topics."
It's not Moved. It's not Convinced. And it doesn't Realize.
On the other hand, it doesn't frown if I write in first-person singular.
It's not an agent. And it doesn't publish.
On the other hand, it doesn't perish.

Further Evil Woman Stanzas

1. The Evil Woman under the Influence
 Oh, the things she has done! The things she will do! Such horrible
    horrible things.
She cares not for man, woman, or child. She cares not for
    God or country.
Fire and brimstone, blood and guts.
Her evil hands will not come unclenched.

2. One Tiny Dream
At night what the evil woman has thought and done becomes
    nightmare.
Blood has become bloodbath. Guts have become gut-spilling.
In the morning she's back to her senses. Only the very last dream
snippet, only that short but intense dream, the one that lingers.
Only that.

3. The Evil Woman Is a Woman
The evil woman, having just given birth
and being in her circles expected to commit infanticide
is thinking, What if?
What if, this time, I don't?
What if I keep this one?
Find out what that's like?
What if I listen to these temporary hormones and take up this baby?

What if I continue to take her? Including take her up,
breastfeed her, clothe her,
rear her, the whole bit.
Can't an evil woman have a child?
And when she's grown, must that child be another evil woman?
Can't an evil woman want better for her child?

4. The Evil Woman in Bodily Pain
She holds onto that part of her body.
She doesn't cry, only winces.
She can still go about her business but chooses not to.
She finds a corner.
She is tough but no tougher than anybody else.

5. The Evil Woman in the Web
"The terrible tangled web we weave
"when first we practice to deceive."
And that was such a long time ago.

6. The Evil Woman at Home
At the end of her evil day she arrives, throws off her evil cloak,
goes into her evil kitchen.
She does not call "Honey, I'm home." There is no Honey.
And there is no home.
She lives alone in her evil nest, a nest without young
a nest which scratches, a nest which rubs it all in.

7. Dream about the Truly Evil Woman
This evil woman won't let me clean my house.
In particular, she won't let me scrub the bathtub.
She keeps grabbing my wrists as I begin to let out the dirty water.
Moreover, into that dirty water she releases a bottle of her evil ink
which settles into an evil face on the bottom just over the drain.
To escape I run out the front door.
It's so easy, I call out, to fly.
And for a while it is
But this time I can't manage higher than five feet.
And the evil woman is more than five feet tall.
Eventually, I go back into the house to talk with her.
How long have you been evil?" "I was an evil baby."
"Why are you evil?" "Because I feel like it."
"I'm afraid of you. Please leave."
But she won't.
She is not like the other evil woman.
I'm looking straight at her but I don't see what she looks like.
I'm afraid she looks like me.
I can only run outside again, this time out the side door.
And this time I don't try to fly.

Portrait of the Mathematician as a New Mother

Devin at three weeks taught me:
there is more than one face.
And given two objects
they probably don't touch.
Devin at three months taught me:
the room is not symmetric.
And six months, Devin
we are all pleading.
At twenty months, every
motion is sweeping.
But, so far he hasn't said anything that hinges on
the value of a distribution at a point
or how to characterize associative arithmetics.
There are many things Devin
taught me to forget.
But the time has now come
to remember.

1995

The Paralyzed Sleep Muscle

Some people can fall asleep any time they want. They can take a nap one hour before bedtime and still sleep again, 8 hours. "I'm feeling sleepy," they say, and then they sleep.

Maybe there's a sleep muscle, a muscle most people have which they move when they decide to sleep, like moving arms or legs. And some people's sleep muscles work better than others.

Where in our bodies are our sleep muscles? And how are we supposed to use them? Some people can wriggle their ears but most people can't. Maybe there's something wrong with my sleep muscle. It's atrophied, paralyzed. Like this woman who had polio as a kid. One of her arms just dangles from her shoulders.

If you could see my sleep muscle, you'd see that it's dangling. Like that woman's arm it needs washing. Or massaging. Or exercising. A physical therapist. But I don't know where it is and neither does any physical therapist. My sleep muscle is a mystery. Inaccessible. Emotionally and physically unavailable. Maybe epileptic.

Or it works when it wants to. It's a separate creature, my conjoined twin. Whether or not I sleep has nothing to do with me.

The Big Bangs Theory

age 16

In "Men of Mathematics" Descartes' face suddenly boomed out.
His hair was long and wavy.
His eyes were large and protruding.
Everything about him was thick and evident.
He looked surprised, maybe scared
as though he'd seen a ghost
or maybe just woken up.
I hesitated to stare at him too often
was afraid somebody would be looking over my shoulder thinking,
"Why is she always staring at Descartes?"

Because he seemed cold, unpopular, and deprived of things like love.
Because he expressed how I felt about math.
And he had bangs.
That's partly what gave him that penetrating look.
Dark curly bangs, pressed against his forehead.
Maybe *glued* to his forehead.
Or growing out of his forehead.
Bangs like fur.
Bangs he couldn't get rid of.
Bangs like a birthmark
inescapably big.

Horton Explores Further

sequel to *Horton Hears a Who*, Dr. Seuss -- from a dream, Oct. 1, 2015

There is a physicist who has proven that there exist universes of infinitesimal size but it's impossible to access them. He nonetheless tries. Spends his life delving into tubes, pipes, various corners of machines, the insides of insides.

But only with long sticks. Very long sticks. Never with his own bare hands. Oh, he doesn't mind getting them dirty. He just doesn't want to get them stuck. So he doesn't want to go too far inside.

Lives

When you see a young woman, you don't know whether
    she'll ever be old.
But when you see an old woman you know she was once young.
She's a known quantity.
She could become even more known.
She could be solved for.
There are enough equations.
Whereas a young woman, no.
Too few equations
too many unknowns.

PART II: Off-Topic

"Does anybody have any fears that they think nobody else has?"

homework and class conversation question about the poem
"Flashcards" by Rita Dove in the course Mathematics in Literature

Crowds. Nicole fears crowds. "I feel like I'm in an area
    I can't get out of."
And timed tests. And any man with a beard. And anything with more
    than four legs.
And cats. "The eyes, the meow noises they make."
And moths. "They flutter around and have no fear of humans."
And falling asleep in cars. That news story about a woman
    sleeping in her car and there was a leak.
And trick or treating. Mike was afraid the person in the house
    wanted to kill children or take them into their houses to never see
    their families again.
Some students have more fears than others.
And some don't tell the class but tell the teacher in their written
    homework.
And, after ten years of this course, there are always new fears.
No end to fears. Every semester new fears.

homework question for Rita Dove's poem, "Flashcards"

Mary Catherine's teacher had bushy eyebrows that made him look angry all the time.

And Mike says, "Coaches seem to have less of a filter than teachers when it comes to personal insults.

Gabby says when she was little, people would ask her, "What do you want to be when you grow up?" Usually the person would ask it in fun and play along when she said chef, astronaut, celebrity. But as she got less little, the question became more serious. They wanted to know what colleges she was applying to and what she would major in. It was a matter of more than wanting. She began to maybe not want to do much of anything when she grew up.

"Which would you prefer, to have made an error or discovered a paradox?"

homework/class conversation question about the story "Division by Zero" in which a mathematician proves without error that 1 = 2, and is very upset

A surprising number of students would rather have discovered a paradox. True, many said, "If I made an error, I could correct it" or "I might feel annoyed with myself, but I could move on." But many others said, "A paradox would be cool," "A paradox would open up a whole new world."

"Paradoxes intrigue my mind," writes Sara. "They make me realize how complex things are and how special the universe is."

And Hannah: "I wouldn't have to blame myself for making the error. I could blame MATH." Yeah, wouldn't students with math anxiety justlove to blame math?! *They* weren't wrong, math was wrong.

All math could be wrong. There could be no such thing as math. No more math, no more anxiety. Hurray for paradoxes! In fact, since everything depends on math, a paradox just might get rid of everything. In particular, everything we're supposed to learn. Everything we might not want to learn. Especially bad things.

Like unexpected tragedies. It couldn't have happened and yet it did, the worst paradox. We could be depressed forever, bargaining forever, denying forever, never reach the acceptance stage, could just keep bargaining, could have both and/or none, could both eat and have our cake, the rest of our lives, forever and ever, once and for all.

Something I'm Proud of

It was 2:00 PM, official dismissal time. Usually I let them go at 1:50 and they're happy when I do. But today they just kept sitting there.

"Hey, you're not giving me any high-sign," I smiled.

They just kept sitting there.

I also kept sitting there, on top of the desk. "Any questions?" No.

So then I asked, "What do you wanna talk about?"

They wanted to talk about their weekend. I'd forgotten to ask about their weekend. And this past weekend was Spring Fling. They wanted to tell me about Spring Fling. Amidst term papers and senior theses, there'd been a carnival, food, dancing.

They truly didn't want to leave my class. I'm proud of that but also sorry I didn't remember to ask about their weekend. They'd had to bring it up. Also, we have only three more classes before the final. I probably didn't want to leave, either.

Sleepy

As though it were, not yesterday, but this morning, I remember the records our parents bought us. In particular "The Sleepy Family". It begins with a lullaby. "My pid- / geon house / is op- / en wide / and I let / my pid- / geons free..." The first non-singing words are "A mother was singing her baby to sleep when in the door walked Father. 'HEL – LO, MOTHER. I THINK... I THINK... A CHOO!' " Next, baby crying, Mother tries various lullabies. "No, that's not baby's song." "That's not baby's song, either." "Oh dear, Father sneezed baby's song clear out of my head."

"But just then, the wi – i – ind ro – o – olled through the trees --- Who -o- o- who-o –o..." ..."and the mother joins in. "They fly / so high / 'til they reach the sky... yes, that's baby's song. Yes, that's it..."

And I begin to tear up. "The wind knew it all the time," and I tear up even more.

"And the song put Baby to sleep

"it put Mother to sleep

"and it even

"put Father to sleep."

I've repeated that record to my first husband, my interim love, and my current. And to my kids, each and all of them and now that they're adults, they ask for it again. But I also think I would like to sing it to my students.

On Final Exam day, in addition to chocolates. "To help you relax," I'd say. I'd sing it and say it and, yes, tear up with it.

"And the song put Baby to sleep

"it put Mother to sleep

"it put Father to sleep

“and it even
“puts
“students to sleep.” The wind knew it all the time.

Not Even Then

Nate last row left says he doesn't like children, didn't even like children when he was a child. "Is there anybody else in the class who didn't like children even when they were children?" Rachel last row right raised her hand. And I have to admit, I like children more now than when I was a child. To me, then, children even just a year older than me looked like adults, they looked as old as my mother, might as well have been wearing lipstick. They were pure peer group, risky, maybe dangerous, not unconditional. Especially in seventh grade.

Devin says when he was a toddler he was shy. Can toddlers be shy? Toddlers seem fine with other toddlers. When adults don't keep interfering, toddlers seem fine together, they *look* fine together, all equally playing, equally talking or not talking, equally climbing and running around. They look just fine, but maybe really they don't like one another, maybe toddlers don't like toddlers.

And maybe roaches don't like roaches, maybe they're just as disgusted by roaches as we are. Roaches seem just fine together. We never see them run from one another, but maybe they do. Maybe everybody's terrified of even their own image.

"If You Like, Write about a Teacher Who Seemed to Be on a Power Trip."

Samantha's tenth-grade teacher assigned the class, write a paper on something you're passionate about. Samantha knew right off she wanted to write about sea glass. But the teacher said, "Why don't you broaden your topic a bit, write about *all* glass?"

Well, Samantha gave it a try, researched all glass and what she found out was, sea glass was the only glass she was the slightest bit interested in, let alone passionate about. So she wrote her paper on only sea glass and she knew it was a good paper but that teacher gave it C, the only C she'd ever gotten, probably because she hadn't taken his suggestion.

I remember sea glass. It's sort of pastel, and translucent, and gentle, not shiny, something like oaktag paper. I too am more passionate about sea glass than any other kind of glass and in this poem I don't want to write about all glass, only sea glass, that's the only glass that makes it into Samantha's paper and into this poem but at least nobody will give this poem a C.

"Do you feel that this story reflects the sexism of the times?"

question for my class about some of our readings
from the 50s

"It's just a story," Luke writes. "I don't care whether it's sexist or not, it's only a story, I don't have to make a big deal about whether it's sexist."

That despite what the students who've taken Feminist Literary Criticism have been saying in class, and what some of the male students have said about wishing they could feel permitted to express their feelings more and despite what I said, that some women really do feel hurt when they see a sexist passage in a story, and especially when they *keep* seeing sexist passages in *lots* of stories.

"I'm not trying to deprive you," I write on Luke's paper, "of any enjoyment you get out of reading the story, I just want to make you aware of the issues involved and I wouldn't have assigned the story if I felt it wasn't a good story in various ways, but I also think the story could have been written in such a way that it was just as good but not sexist."

Well, Luke, maybe the next sexist story but nope, the next one he writes "I told you, it's just a story, I'm not going to answer that question, I'll answer all the other questions but not that one. It's just a story, just a story."

The Lives of Some Young People

Samantha has a genetic progressive disease affecting joints, muscles and head. So she can't do sports which she loved more than anything else, then and since. "I probably won't miss any class because of it", she writes on her Friendly Questionnaire, but on the third week she got an especially bad migraine and also on the fourth. And she keeps on keeping on, studying, attending classes, doing homework, making up homework, planning a career and a life. She sits next to her friends and giggles during groupwork, doesn't want any special treatment, only accommodations, she works hard, has white-blonde hair, wears Free People clothes, will be making Thanksgiving dinner in her dorm room with her friend, will keep on keeping on.

A Childhood

"Do you think Mrs. Torry had a regular childhood?" –
homework question for the story "An Old Arithmetician"

Sienna tells us when she was a kid, she was afraid of the other kids, they were so big. She said her sister went outside all the time but she never wanted to, and when she was bad her parents didn't ground her, they did the very opposite, they sent her outside.

Not to worry, she'd bring a book and find a quiet hidden spot. Like the little bird in that poem, "the north wind doth blow / and we shall have snow / and what will the robin do then / poor thing. / He'll sit in a barn / to keep himself warm / and hide his head under his wing / poor thing."

Yes, hide his head under his wing.

"Have any of you, if you want to share this, ever thought about committing suicide?"

question that came up in class while studying the story,
"Young Archimedes" by Aldous Huxley, in which
a six-year-old commits suicide

When Violet was six years old, she decided she wanted to die because then she might be reincarnated into a cat. Cats are so pretty, and they don't do all the mean things humans do, they might do all the mean things cats do but those things wouldn't be as bad. If she were a cat she wouldn't have to play outside with kids her own age and she wouldn't have to go to school, all she'd have to do was be a cat.

But then she realized she didn't know how to make herself die and also, she wouldn't be able to be her parents' child or play with her favorite toys or find out what would happen with the rest of her life.

Last

The last day of the last Math/Lit semester was great, we read poems, our own, others', any poems we wanted. We laughed, we lamented, re-bonded. But in the dream the last day was even better. One of the students sang a song she'd written, a song instead of a poem, like once in real-life a student did her math-poem critique on a song, "songs are sort of like poems," she wrote and hm, maybe songs are better than poems. In the dream the student's song made the whole class cry, teacher too. We all kept crying and we asked whether she'd written other songs and she had, she kept singing her songs and we kept crying. Then another student said she also wrote songs. Poems made us laugh and lament, but songs made us cry. I should teach songs instead of poems, should write songs instead of poems, I should and I do dream songs instead of poems, at least every once in a while.

Way Off-Topic

All of a sudden half the class was shouting across the room "I HATED gym." – "I hated gym, too." – "I REALLY hated gym." – "Oh? Did YOU hate gym? Me too." It had somehow come up, even though it was history teachers Kieshyna had said she hated. Maybe they all, or they some, had already heard from their friends who'd taken the course that it's okay to talk (or shout across the room) about things like hating gym.

Every class is different and this time it was unanimous, nobody called out "Hey wait a sec, I LOVED gym." I let them keep it up and then said, "In a couple weeks we'll have more opportunity to talk about things like hating gym."

We'd had enough for now.

Students Share about the Day after the 2016 Election

Lanibel, Heather, and Imani were each accosted by other students, enemies and friends, maliciously or jokingly. "You're an alien. Trump's gonna deport you." They each gave up those friends. But they couldn't give up those enemies.

And Lauren and six of her friends – "and we're all geeky and gay", she tells us – were commiserating together in the school cafeteria and a bunch of tough guys – "football player types," Lauren said -- sauntered over to their table and drawled, "Trump says you don't belong here, get out."

Nobody else was around, it had been very quiet all throughout the school on that day, even the cafeteria workers were too far away to see what was going on, and Lauren and her friends were very, very scared. They didn't fight back, with fists or with words, they didn't call Security, and they didn't report anything, they just got out.

What about the civility flag? Didn't Arcadia raise their Civility flag?"

The kids all shrugged. "Probably Security would've backed those guys up. Those guys are probably big sports stars or something." These students don't trust cafeteria workers, don't trust Security, don't trust the Civility flag, just plain don't trust.

"When you're going through stressful times, what helps?"

question that came up while discussing my memoir,
"The Night I Almost Didn't Grow Up"

Not math, not literature, not their major, not their friends. Rather, says Heather, her service dog. Because she has anxiety disorder, she's allowed to have a pet in her dorm room. Oh yes, pipes up Lauren, her service dog's the light of her life, too. And so is Kelly's and so is Bryn's. And the whole class turns around to that back row, and everybody takes out their computers and brings up screen-sized photos of their pets. Cats, dogs, and Caylie tells us her roommate has a service rat, she'd sworn she'd never think of that rat as a pet but now she says he's the cutest thing ever.

What ELSE helps? Heather raises her hand again. Piercings. Yup, every time things get tough it's time for another piercing. Lauren agrees. And then they start talking about tattoos, when things get tough the tough get another tattoo. "For some people," says Lauren, "the ones that hurt the most are in places that are fatty like the underside of your arm. But for some people those are the less painful places, and the most painful are just over a bone, like along your spine." "They hurt, but they're worth it," puts in Heather. "It's worth it," she repeats.

And so I listen and learn and now I don't have to get a tattoo or piercing since now I know all about them. Thanks, guys.

"For the non-math-lovers: Is there any part of math that you do love?"

Emma would get addicted to any problem involving knight moves, Helen and her corner loved that trick for multiplying, and lots of students hated geometry but loved algebra, or vice versa.

And now Teddy tells us he likes squares, not the shapes but numbers multiplied by themselves. When he can't think of anything else to do he calculates squares. And he's beginning to work on cubes, then he'll work his way to fourth and fifth powers.

And when I need to relax and still want to do something math-like, I play solitaire at the kitchen table. I like the way it looks, red under black under red, n+1 under n and I like it when I can turn over a card and find out what lies beneath. I could think about the more interesting problem of what's the probability of winning solitaire but I'm not going there, I'm just plain-old *playing* the game, maybe three or four times, just before bedtime when I don't feel like reading and can't think of anything else to do.

Fears, Fall 2017

"If you like, share any fears that you have that you feel
most people don't have?"
--- homework question for the poem "Flashcards" by Rita
Dove

Shani's the first to raise her hand for that question. She's, well, not
exactly *afraid* of grass, she just doesn't *walk* on it. Especially in bare feet.
Who knows what lurks inside grass? If there was a bug in there, or a razor
blade, she wouldn't know 'til she stepped on it? And if there was a big
hole in the earth, grass might be covering it.

She doesn't walk on dirt either.

Strictly concrete. What she sees is what she walks on.

What she walks on is what she gets.

Just a Little Cat

Katie couldn't solve the trees riddle, on her paper were pretty attempts, 9 lines, 5 dots on each, too much more than 19, total. But she doodled.

And one thing she doodled was the cutest kitten I'd ever seen. No correct point and line configuration, nothing I could give her extra credit for. Only a little cat, just sitting there on top of her page, pudgy body, chubby paws, endearing tail-end peeking out from behind. "Oh, I love that cat," I told her, "I *want* that cat" and she smiled, "you can have it."

She handed me her paper without the riddle solution, and I took it because I wanted that cat, I still have it. I couldn't give her extra credit for it, I don't give a class participation grade, but when I made up the final semester grades, I couldn't forget it, couldn't forget that cute little cat.

The Colors of Everything

One of the students has synesthesia and is proud of and happy about it. What color is 3? we ask her. Green, she says. Yes, we agree, 3 is green and what color is 4? Yellow.

And not only numbers. Love? we ask. Pink, she answers, and so do we. And God? Some of us are believers, some not, but we all know God's color is light-blue like the sky. In other words, the whole class has synesthesia. Maybe we're not as good at it as the student who bona fide has it but we're good. Proud and happy too.

PART III: Mourning Pluto

Mourning the Dream

82

When Devin was twelve he had one of those 45-minute dreams that seemed like 45 years. He dreamt he was married with kids, he dreamt his wife, he dreamt each kid. When he woke up... well, he'd never before minded not being an adult but now he missed his wife and kids. And it was already 7:00 AM, time to get up for school, no time to keep missing his wife and kids.

"Stuart Little"

My little sister ran downstairs crying. "He didn't find her. He never found her."

Our mother received her with open arms. "Oh," she said. "I'm sure he did. The book *said* he was sure he would. That's one of those implied endings. It doesn't actually say he found her, it just says he knows he will."

But my sister went on crying. She wanted her happy ending in black and white, wanted to see it happen, read it happen, read it proven, given and proven, he found her, he found her, Q.E.D.

Very Young

title inspired by Anne Sexton's "Young"

- Foreign people were very quiet and blonde.
  They wore sunbonnets, fully gathered skirts, and wooden shoes.
  Foreign children never chanted "No more teachers' dirty looks"
  nor snickered "This place is saved, and not for you."
  And Jeanette van Dyke and Peter van Gilder didn't adjust beautifully to the Harrison School dialect but played only with each other, sometimes even alone.
- Poor people lived in huts and never left home.
  Mother, father, and children ate from one big wooden bowl and
    huddled on one straw mat.
  Poor teenagers didn't slink around street corners, snap rock 'n'
    roll, or sport makeup.
  And if we ever reached a point where we didn't know what to do
    next, we could always be poor.
- Thinking people were sad, not bitter.
  Misanthropes were waiting for the right human being to come
    along.
  Atheists minded there not being a God. Solipsists minded there
    not being anybody else.
  Poets didn't socialize with other poets.

Mathematicians didn't tell in-jokes.
Existentialists didn't have all those love affairs.
Thinking people didn't ever forget what they'd thought.
Thinking people sat in rooms all day and cried.

Music Listening Room, NYU

Freshman year, fall semester, the second movement of Beethoven's Seventh recognized me. I told my mother about it. "It's dark, like the bottom of the universe. Or like someone trying to press down on that bottom, trying to make it go even lower."

But my mother said only, "it's very sexual." And I thought, "Is that all?"

"Does anyone want to share any truths in their lives that were or are precious to them and that they needed or need to defend?"

homework question for the story "Inflexible Logic"

When Frank was in grammar school, he loved making models of the solar system, nine spheres rotating and revolving, different sizes, different colors, he loved the solar system, the way it was, the way we all thought it was, and that solar system was Frank's precious truth.

Well, he got over it, got used to the truncated solar system, but it wasn't easy, was kind of a big deal for a little kid, and he defended his truth-turned-untruth by denial, his models kept on having nine.

And then Kaylee knew all about it, how what we thought was a planet is really a dwarf planet and not even a particularly special one, how there are hundreds of dwarf planets and I quipped, "See, Frank, you didn't lose a planet, you gained hundreds of dwarf planets," and we all laughed, Frank too. Indeed, he's gotten over it, but of course.

The Hole

Down our childhood cellar was a hole in the left wall, small enough not to break the wall but large enough for my sister and me to climb through. We didn't worry about dirt or bugs, just climbed through the hole and dropped under the front porch. We got to see the underside of steps, the pink sides of those formidable cement blocks. We sat down in separate corners and said, "Just think, we're in the hole."

And then we didn't know what else to say or do. We could bring a blanket and have a picnic in there, we could lie down on the blanket and take a nap in there, we could bring flashlights and draw pictures in there, we could pretend it was a little house and live in there. We could... we could... oh come on, there had to be *something*.

The Next-Best Doll

The best doll had everything a doll could have, real blonde curly hair, rosy cheeks, pink dress, white leather shoes, and she came in a transparent box which displayed all her accessories, purse, comb and brush, alternate dresses, and shoes. And Aunt Faygie said she'd buy it for us.

But then she saw the price tag, even Aunt Faygie with a fulltime librarian job and no children couldn't afford it. So instead we got Bonnie, as big as the best doll, but coming with only one outfit and it wasn't a dress, and no accessories, and no rosy cheeks or hair, real or pretend. She was a bald, relatively naked doll.

That's what we got instead.

The Definition of Almost

This must have been a dream, it's so illogical, my mother said,
  "On Monday you'll be almost five."
I didn't hear that "almost."
I counted the days and on Monday I woke up all-excited.
"I'm five! I'm five!"
But my mother said, "No, I said *almost* five."
I don't remember turning actual-five.
Maybe I thought actual was just another almost.

How to Tell the Kids

91

At some point in our growing our parents told us the good news, meaning the facts of life, how the baby gets into the mother's stomach.

But who tells us the bad news, those other facts of life, and of death, like war, slavery, holocaust, capital punishment? Maybe they *don't* tell us. Maybe that news is so bad they can't bear to tell us. We have to find it out for ourselves.

Fall Back

This morning there's a kind of jetlag.
The buses are too crowded.
They're on the same schedule but something's different.
This natural light doesn't look natural.
Daylight is being spent rather than saved.
What worked for Sunday night doesn't work for Monday morning
and 7:30 AM will have trouble being 7:30 AM
for at least a little while.

Homeroom

In fifth grade, even though you start having too many classrooms,
you have the same homeroom four times a day.
In seventh grade you have homeroom twice a day.
In ninth grade once a day.
In college no homeroom at all.
You wander from class to class, building to building, through
    shadows of buildings and you don't have homeroom.
Sometimes you feel homesick.
When you're a college professor, you don't have homeroom.
You have an office and after class you run to it.
You arrive breathless with hat and coat, flop down in your big
    rolling chair but there's no homeroom teacher.
You fling open your door, make the four walls three.
You hit your books, papers, computer.
You keep glancing at that doorway and the hallway beyond, and
    it's not your office hours and you're not in homeroom.
Sometimes you still feel homesick.

Work Ethics

At the supper table one evening our father once reflected, "Gee, I'm tired of being a high school teacher. Fifteen years is an awfully long time and American history is an awfully boring subject."

At this point, I'm sure, he winked at our mother.

"I think I'll quit,' he continued. "I think I'll call them up tomorrow morning and tell them I'm going to a different job."

At this point, now that I remember, our mother winked back.

"Well, kids, whaddaya say?" he concluded. "Whaddaya think I should be?"

"Ooo, ooo, Daddy, be a toy salesman! Then we can get a lot of toys."

"No, be a TV producer, then we can be on TV."

"No, never mind. Be the leader of the bank. Then we'll be rich."

"Hmm," our father mused. 'Very interesting suggestions. Before you go to bed tonight, let me know if you have any more so I can sleep on it and get to my new job bright and early tomorrow morning."

By the time we were tucked in we had thought of fireman, postman, and staying a teacher but transferred to our school.

And instead of a glass of water we came downstairs three times to tell him about movie star, Santa Claus, and child psychologist.

All that night we wondered and dreamed about which one he'd choose and the next morning we ran downstairs all legs and ears.

At the breakfast table, however --

"Well, kids, thank you very much for all your wonderful ideas. I've thought them over very carefully and I've decided that what I really like best is being a history teacher at Perth Amboy High School."

"Aw Daddy."

“Come ON.”

“We might’ve known.”

We really believed he could quit his job whenever he wanted.

Really believed he could pick something more exciting and go to it right away.

Really believed he could buy a toy factory, take over the bank, or show up to the right of Buffalo Bob one day and offer to help out.

We really believed he had a choice

and were disappointed in him for not making it.

High-School Reunion Dreams

It's as though you arrived late.
The crowds have already formed.
Every once in a while you see a new arrival. Wow, here's your
    big chance.
But she just runs over to one of the crowds.
That happens many times.
In another dream nobody recognizes anybody else.
They're all sitting by themselves.
You move among these sitters, making an attempt.
But each briefly mumbles something unintelligible, then
    begins to bend down.
This is a boring high-school reunion but at least we're having it.
At least we're getting to find out.

If I Hadn't Skipped First Grade

If I hadn't skipped first grade, I'd've had one more year to learn carrying and borrowing.

If I hadn't skipped first grade, I'd've gone one more year without changing classes and term reports and men teachers.

And one more year without knowing about homework and lipstick and stockings.

A few days after skipping first grade, I peered through auditorium doors.

The stage was lit up like the sky, with grass and rainbows and pastel flowers the height of children. Oh, how I wanted to walk through those doors, but it was the first grade's turn for assembly that day and I'd been in first grade on the second grade's day.

If I hadn't skipped first grade, I'd be one year younger.

If I hadn't skipped first grade, I'd still be a child.

One Thing Missing

I got a lot of closure out of my 50-year high school reunion. I was second-in-command as organizer, buddy-buddy with the first-in-command, asked to do a reunion-related poetry reading, and someone said, "and you made it –- Ph.D., two husbands, four children, 19 books", and somebody else said, "NOBODY in those days felt popular," and the most popular girl in the class said, "your poems made me cry." But I still think it would have done me good, in the remaining years of my life, if some boy, any boy, had confessed to me, over or after the reunion dinner, "You know, I had a big crush on you those four years." Yes, that would have been more closure, would have done me more good.

Just Because

Just because we remember as though it were yesterday and just because we remember yesterday doesn't mean we won't die. We'll wind up precisely like those who *don't* remember as though it were yesterday. One difference, though: we won't die wondering, we'll die remembering.

The Staten Island Ferry

There already had been and have been since
incidents that break the faith in the order of the universe.
But this is the one I'm remembering right now:
 I had ridden several times on the Staten Island Ferry
mostly in single-digit years, doubly enclosed in the ferry and
      my parents' black Pontiac
but also in double-digit years, a few times, enclosed in only
      it and free to wander.
I had wished the ride could last longer than five minutes.
Motion so slow, view changing so slightly, almost tantalizingly.
And the choices we had – to stand or to sit, and where –
In the five minutes I made sure to sample all the choices.
And the floor so thick, so deep.
This boat seemed as sturdy as a planet.
I lost my faith in safety when some radio hissed the news
there'd been an accident
people killed.
How can you die in five minutes?
How could something deeper than the sea sink?
How could a whole planet collide?
How could something moving so slowly move wrong?
 I didn't catch the details, nor did I try.
I only noted
in a different way from before
that if the Staten Island Ferry could betray
if the Staten Island Ferry could be overcome

could lose a war that was never declared
then no container could protect.
Even if it wasn't moving.
Even if it was still as a house.
Bad things can happen even without motion.
I used to think *nothing* could happen without motion.
That was one of my early-adolescent theories.
I hadn't had silly theories like that in a long time.
But when that news came over the radio
I mourned my old silly theories.
And I mourned the Staten Island Ferry
and those magic five-minute rides
as magic as dreams.
I knew I would never dream like that again.

Who Is Sylvia?

In the dream I'm listening to the song and crying.
When I wake up I'm still crying.
Not because my mother's name was Sylvia.
But because I was friends with neither Schubert nor Shakespeare
so that beautiful song wasn't written for me.

The Theory of Complementary Objects

Every object has its own unique set of properties.

No two distinct objects have the same set of properties.

So we can *define* an object as a set of properties.

And we can define a *sub-object* as a subset of the
   object's properties.

And then the *complement* of an object as the negations of that
   object's properties.

Also, an object is said to *exist* if it contains, for each property,
   either that property or its negation, and not both.

The theory breaks down pretty quickly.

For example, what about the property of not being capable of riding
   a bicycle?

And what about the universal object which is the set of all properties?

Or the poor non-existent null object

with no properties at all?

*Photo by Marielle Joy
Cohen*

About the Author

Marion Deutsche Cohen is known, in particular, for her writings (poetry and memoir) on three topics: spousal chronic illness, late pregnancy loss, and math. She is the author of 33 books; her newest poetry collection is *Negative Aspects* (dancing girl press), and her latest prose collection is *Not Erma Bombeck: Diary of a Feminist 70s Mother* (Alien Buddha Press). Forthcoming is *Reasons and Remedies for Insomnia* (dancing girl press). She is also the author of two controversial memoirs about spousal chronic illness, a trilogy diary of full-term-pregnancy loss, and *Crossing the Equal Sign,* about the experience of and her passion for math. She teaches a course she developed, Mathematics in Literature, at Drexel University's Honors College. Other poetic inspirations are classical piano, singing, Scrabble®, thrift-shopping, four grown children, two grown step-children, and six grands. Her website is marioncohen.net.

Image owned by the
artist.

About the Artist

Devin Asher Cohen multi-instrumentalist, multidisciplinary artist, works with experimental abstract visual art, painting, poetry, sound art, and has written, painted, exhibited, performed, across the U.S., Mexico, Israel, Paris, Iceland, Germany, Sweden, Lithuania, Spain, Japan, Hungary, Greece... His poetry book is ALL PRAISES and his experimental Alien Architect trip hop post hop poetry album is Arteria. He has attended artist residencies in Hungary, Lithuania, Romania... His work has been selected for the Ibero Biennale de Puebla de Los Ángeles, as well as the Biennale de pintura J.A. Monroy in Mexico. Devin's work has been exhibited in Museo de Arte Contemporáneo Ateneo de Yucatán MACAY, Centro Estatal de las Artes de Baja California in Tijuana, Centro Cultural Plaza Fatima in Monterrey, Museo UPAEP in Puebla, Museo de la Mujer in Mexico City, as well as the Slought Foundation and Barnes Foundation in Philadelphia. Devin Cohen and his partner Rebeca Martel own and curate Liliput Gallery in Puebla, Mexico, and Philiput Gallery in Philadelphia, Pennsylvania, USA.